PROSPERO'S LIBRARY

The Book of

Dream Symbols

PAVILION

The Book of Dream Symbols
First published in Great Britain in 1994 by

PAVILION BOOKS LIMITED
26 Upper Ground, London SE1 9PD

A DBP Book, conceived, edited and designed by Duncan Baird Publishers
Highlight House, 57 Margaret Street, London W1N 7FG

Text: *Peter Bently*
Design: *Karen Wilks*
Commissioned artwork/photography:
*Nick Bell, Ian Craig, Peter Crowther, Richard Jenkins, Sheena Land,
Emma Parker, Paul Redgrave, Peter Till, Steve Wallace*
See page 40

A CIP catalogue record for this book is available from
The British Library

ISBN 1 85793 1440

2 4 6 8 10 9 7 5 3 1

This book may be ordered by post from the publisher.
Please contact the Marketing Department.
But try your local bookshop first.

Contents

The stuff of dreams

The psychoanalyst Sigmund Freud (1856-1939) said that to unlock the secret symbolism of our dreams we need look no further than ourselves. Filtered through the unconscious, our most profound experiences are presented back to us in scrambled form.

Distortions

The size of things in dreams will often be determined by factors such as their importance in our lives. We may dwarf the world around us (a possible indication of egocentricity); or everyday objects may become terrifyingly huge, as they seemed in childhood.

Time and space

In a few seconds of dreaming we can live through hours, weeks, years or a lifetime. A dream may take us backward or forward in time to encounter ancestors, historical figures, our younger or older selves, even unborn generations. Locations can also shift abruptly, transporting us from the comfort of a familiar room to some foreign city or dizzy mountain precipice.

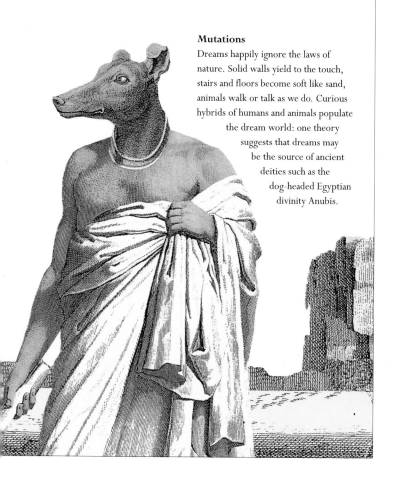

Mutations

Dreams happily ignore the laws of
nature. Solid walls yield to the touch,
stairs and floors become soft like sand,
animals walk or talk as we do. Curious
hybrids of humans and animals populate
the dream world: one theory
suggests that dreams may
be the source of ancient
deities such as the
dog-headed Egyptian
divinity Anubis.

The archetypes

Freud's pupil Carl Gustav Jung (1875-1961) identified a number of archetypes, or "structural elements of the psyche". These are the basic ingredients of the unconscious, symbolized in dreams by various images drawn from the conscious world.

Animus and anima

The animus, the male side of the female persona, represents "masculine" qualities, such as courage and rationality. In dreams it could be symbolized by a white knight or by a modern counterpart such as a detective hero. The anima, the female side of the male persona, represents "female" qualities, such as compassion and emotionality. In dreams it may appear as a mother figure or as a powerful personality, such as the biblical Judith.

Great Mother and Wise Old Man

The Great Mother is the entirety of the female persona. Its aspects include the "Angry Goddess" (possessive and destructive), the "Princess" (warm and loving) and the "Amazon" (intellectual and ambitious). The Wise Old Man is the whole male persona. Its aspects include the "Ogre" (authoritarian and conformist), the "Hero" (aggressive and strong-willed) and the "Trickster" (unpredictable and elusive) (above).

Shadow

Deep in the unconscious lurks the Shadow, the dark side of the conscious persona. It may be alarming for the dreamer to encounter a cruel, self-centred alter ego. But we are all capable of evil: to recognize this makes it less likely that the Shadow will torment us with its repressed urges.

The whole self

Jung defined the Self as "the totality of the psyche". Encompassing the dreamer's entire personality, it comprises both conscious and subconscious minds. The Self is symbolized in dreams in many forms: one is the *mandala*, a geometrical emblem containing a distinct focal point, like the device used for meditation in Eastern mysticism.

Mirror
Meeting our reflection in a mirror suggests a desire to see ourselves as others do, perhaps as part of a broader search for self-knowledge. It also warns about pushing the search too far: beware of narcissism!

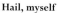

Hail, myself

An encounter with one's *doppelgänger*, or double,
is traditionally held to be an omen of death;
in dreams it is likely to reveal an awareness
of mortality. Meeting yourself as a baby
or child suggests a desire for the security
of early years, while a meeting with
the aged self may express deep-seated
worries for the future. A *doppelgänger*
who behaves in an uncharacteristically
menacing way probably represents
the dreamer's Shadow, or sinister
alter ego.

Pole

The North and South Poles define the
axis around which the world revolves,
just as the Self is the axis of the dreamer's
persona. Searching for the pole
in a dream implies a quest for
the true focal point of the
personality, the starting point
for its future development.

Metamorphoses

Since ancient times, shape-changing has had a powerful hold on the imagination. A dream metamorphosis may reveal basic aspects of the Self: for example, the dreamer may turn into a creature or person showing characteristics of one of the Jungian archetypes.

Wild beast

If the dreamer becomes a powerful animal, such as a lion, tiger or bull, this may reflect a struggle to get inside (and thereby overcome) what Jung called "the animal instincts of the unconscious". Or it could indicate a subconscious fear of one's own raw physical power, especially within a sexual relationship.

Role-playing

Transformation into another person can reveal much about our self-image. For example, to become an actor or actress suggests a suspicion that we are not presenting our true face to the world. Cleopatra may represent the archetype of the Great Mother, while Shakespeare could stand for the Wise Old Man – although such important historical figures could also indicate that the dreamer is prey to egotism.

The self and others

Dreams reveal how, from the earliest age, other people have defined our individuality. The relationship of child, mother and father is the most fundamental influence on the formation of the Self. The anonymous mass of fellow humanity is another powerful shaping force.

Family

Members of the family usually stand
for themselves or for the attributes they
represent and have helped to shape in
the dreamer, such as motherhood. If
the whole family appears, the dreamer
may be trying to shake off the influence
of father, mother or a sibling by submerging
him or her in the wider group.

Ancestors

If ancestors appear in a dream, this may reflect a search for higher moral or
spiritual values, especially if the dreamer assumes an ancestor's identity. Such
dreams may also reveal an attempt to probe as deeply as possible into the recesses
of the Self, in search of what Jung called our "innate psychic disposition".

Crowds

If, in a dream, we see ourselves as part of
a great throng, this may indicate a desire
to assume a more anonymous role in life,
shaking off worries and responsibilities
that have become too great a burden.
If everyone is staring at us, we
may be worried about making
a bad impression on others.

Love and passion

Freud never believed, as is popularly supposed, that all dreams have a sexual content. However, he did claim that love and sex lay at the root of much dream symbolism and asserted that any idea or image was capable of representing the dreamer's erotic behaviour and desires.

Fruit

The apple is associated with the classical love goddess Venus and with Eve's temptation of Adam. In dreams, apples can also represent breasts and hence the dreamer's mother. Peaches and similarly shaped fruit represent the female genitalia.

Fish

The fish, an ancient and highly potent symbol, is associated with the depths of the unconscious. In dreams a fish may reflect a man's sexual urges or a fear that he will lose his virility.

Bees

These restless insects,
linked with love and fertility
since ancient times, express both
the aspirations and the doubts of the
dreamer in love. We hope our efforts will
bring sweet results – but we are also aware
that we might be stung.

Running water

Water in general is associated with the force
of life and generative power. Gushing water
is said to denote the sense of release associated
with orgasm.

Flowers

A common emblem of
blossoming or, if the flowers
are withered, declining love.
Fallen petals may symbolize the
dreamer's feelings about the
prospect (or reality) of losing
his or her virginity.

Hope and ambition

Dreams reveal our most deeply felt aims and aspirations. A race may symbolize the urgency with which we wish to see our goals fulfilled. Walls can stand for obstacles that threaten to thwart our ambitions. Symbols such as the Holy Grail, the cup or bowl used by Christ at the Last Supper, point to hopes and yearnings of the highest spiritual kind.

Rainbow
According to the ancient dream writers, rainbows presage good fortune. However, they are believed today to contain a possible warning against overambition. Jung wrote: "Only the gods can walk rainbow bridges in safety ... for the rainbow is just a lovely semblance which spans the sky, and not a highway for human beings."

Heavenly ladder

The ladder between the earth and the heavens expresses the dreamer's aspirations to a higher level of spiritual or material attainment. In the Bible, Jacob dreams of a stairway to Heaven; from the top of it God promises Jacob that his descendants will inherit the land of Israel.

Gold

Alchemists spent centuries searching in vain for the mystical "philosopher's stone" that would turn base metals into precious gold. Gold symbolizes the dreamer's highest material aspirations, with the implication that they might be unattainable.

Temple

Temples and other places of worship are often designed as microcosms – that is, miniature representations of the cosmos. In dreams, they can symbolize the pursuit and achievement of creative and spiritual goals.

Dangers and demons

Behind the closed doors of the mind lurk the dark forces that encroach upon the dreamer's hopes and happiness. Dreams can open these doors, presenting anxieties and uncertainties as concrete images from the waking world. For example, a pirate or other disreputable figure may symbolize the suppressed guilt assailing the dreamer's conscience.

Unknown waters

Seas and lakes may represent the unfathomed depths of the mind, where our anxieties and untested capacity for evil lie hidden. Freud, though, believed that water often symbolizes a craving for the safety of the womb.

Vampires
The bloodsucking demon that takes the form of a bat to feed on the sleeping victim may represent fear or guilt in the face of excessive or illicit (even incestuous) sexual desires.

Horned creatures
Beasts with horns, such as goats, bulls or even horned beetles, were once linked with the sinister side of phallic power, as embodied in figures such as the Devil and the Greek god Pan. However, in modern times these creatures may be seen to represent male sexual potency as a positive, creative force.

Sharpened weapons
Knives, swords or other blades could be a warning of suicidal tendencies or a secret death wish toward someone else. For the older dream writers, these symbols meant that death, deceit, indifference or misunderstanding threatened to cut off close friends or loved ones.

The dreamer in motion

Dreams of unusual activity, such as floating in mid-air, can express our innermost feelings. The ancients recognized the import of such dreams: Artemidorus of Daldis claimed that trying to run but being unable to move meant that "your goals would be hard to achieve".

Glued to the spot

Striving to run but getting nowhere could represent an attempt to flee some powerful inner urge. The dreamer may harbour secret desires but be restrained by fear or shame from pursuing them.

Flying

Dreams of levitation are the
ultimate expression of a desire to leave
the earthly routine and be as free as a bird.
They could also denote soaring ambition.

Falling

To dream of falling is said to be a sign of anxiety
and vulnerability or an omen of misfortune.
This dream can also represent
yielding to the control of
another: for example, it may
symbolize sexual intercourse.

Landing

The earth is a symbol of fertility
and therefore of coupling – so hitting
the ground points to worries about a sexual
relationship. A soft landing (for example, on
flowers) indicates optimism about the outcome;
a hard landing, the opposite.

Omen and prophecy

A few days before his murder, Abraham
Lincoln dreamed that the White House was
in mourning for an assassinated president.
Given proven cases such as this, it is
understandable that modern
psychology has not eradicated
the traditional belief in the
prophetic power of dreams.

The shower of fortune

A gentle or sudden shower
is said by some writers on
dreams to ensure prosperity
in business and good
fortune at sea. Rain may
also signal an end to a
barren period in the
dreamer's intellectual
or emotional life.

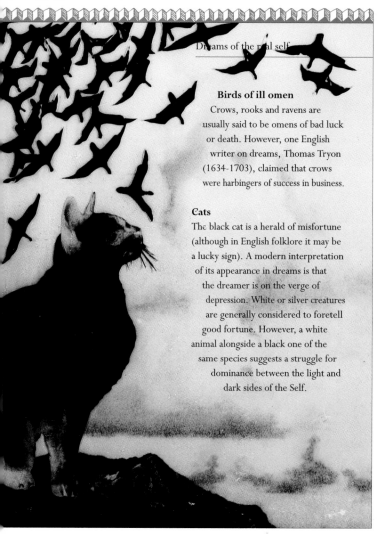

Birds of ill omen

Crows, rooks and ravens are usually said to be omens of bad luck or death. However, one English writer on dreams, Thomas Tryon (1634-1703), claimed that crows were harbingers of success in business.

Cats

The black cat is a herald of misfortune (although in English folklore it may be a lucky sign). A modern interpretation of its appearance in dreams is that the dreamer is on the verge of depression. White or silver creatures are generally considered to foretell good fortune. However, a white animal alongside a black one of the same species suggests a struggle for dominance between the light and dark sides of the Self.

Children's dreams

Because children do not have an adult's grasp of language and imagery it is not always easy to interpret their accounts of their own dreams. However, a child's dreams tend to reflect the jumble of new impressions that a young person encounters each day on the path to knowledge and self-awareness.

Families
Bold geometrical shapes suggest a preoccupation with certain relationships within the family, such as the triangle of father, mother and child. There is no need to be too alarmed at violence done to a parent in an older child's dream: the child is probably overdramatizing a growing need for independence.

Teacher
A male teacher represents male authority and may reflect the child's concern about its relationship with its father, especially if the teacher resembles the parent.

Land of the giants

A child's impression of its size can reflect its sense of self-worth. Everything naturally seems bigger to a child than it does to an adult; but if a child takes on giant proportions in comparison with the surrounding world, its self-awareness could be increasing at a precocious rate.

Toys

A child's toys can come startlingly to life during sleep as the child lives out its fantasies. Some toys could denote developing aspects of the young dreamer's persona: a doll, for example, may symbolize a girl's growing sense of her own femininity.

Nature

The landscape furnishes dreams with powerful metaphors for the body and various aspects of the psyche. A spring can symbolize the fount of life and therefore the focus of the inner Self. A ploughed field could stand for motherhood and an uncut meadow for virginity. A deep valley may represent the womb.

Mountains

Life's challenges can present themselves in dreams as hills and mountains: the steeper the slope, the greater the challenge. As early as c.350AD, the Greek writer Astrampsychus claimed that "to creep up a mountain signifies the difficulties of business".

Rivers

A river symbolizes life and the development of the Self. From small beginnings in the womb of the earth, it runs through many twists, meanders, torrents, falls and shallows, growing broader, deeper and slower as it approaches the end of its course.

Lakes

A secluded lake may represent some aspect of our persona we are seeking to learn more about. If, in a dream, a river flows into a lake, we could be trying to grasp what lies beyond the natural course of our lives.

Gardens

A symbol of the inner life and the qualities the dreamer may be cultivating, a garden can also be a *mandala*, or geometrical emblem of the Self, especially if it is enclosed and contains a focal point such as a fountain.

Trees

The tree is an ancient emblem of life and growth. It is also a phallic symbol and in a man's dream may reflect concerns about sexual or physical potency. In the Book of Daniel, the King of Babylon recounts one such dream: "an holy one came down from heaven; He cried aloud … 'Hew down the tree, and cut off his branches.' "

Flame and flood

Fire and water, two of nature's four elements, tend to represent powerful forces within ourselves, such as sexual drive or maternal instincts. Because they are irreconcilable – fire evaporates water and water extinguishes flame – both elements occurring in the same dream may reflect some great inner conflict.

Fire

Fire is the heat of passion and lust, and a blaze raging out of control expresses our emotions at their most unpredictable and destructive. In a dream, our decision to fight or flee a conflagration could reveal our ability or inability to confront our most extreme feelings. But fire also means light, warmth and security (the hearth) and can be a purifying force that clears out dead wood, opens new vistas and lights the way through the dark forests of life.

Water

Dreams of deep, murky and turbulent
waters may represent the unconscious,
unformed Self on which our conscious
persona rests. Like fire, water stands
for the destructive forces within us —
as in dreams of devastating floods —
but it can also be a cleansing, purifying
element. Rivers are symbols of the
peaceful flow of life toward some
material or inner goal. Immersion may
symbolize a desire for a return to the
womb or for spiritual renewal.

Buildings

As the body is sometimes referred to as a house for the soul, so a house or other building can stand for the dreamer: behind the public façade of the outer persona are the dark, unexplored closets and secret chambers of the mind. The style of architecture may say something about our basic attitudes, from the moral stolidity of Victorian to the unrestrained exuberance of Baroque.

Basements and cellars

Jung had a dream in which he descended deeper and deeper into the basement of his family home, discovering a series of cellars, each more ancient than the last. The dream, he concluded, was an odyssey through the many layers of experience that made up his conscious persona.

Doorways and entrances
Freud said that, for some dreamers, a door or other
entrance "stands for one of the bodily orifices". But while
the act of passing through a door and into a hallway may be
open to sexual interpretation, it could also suggest that the
way out of some personal difficulty lies close before us.

Windows
In a dream, a window may have similar symbolism to a
doorway; however, it can also be a way of recognizing
our true outlook on the world. A pessimistic dreamer
might look through a window onto a bleak and barren
landscape, whereas an optimist might find the view bright
and verdant. Windows are also the means by which light
may be shed on our unconscious anxieties and aspirations.

Stairs and ladders
According to Jung, climbing steps
and ladders hints at "the process
of psychic transformation, with all
its ups and downs". Ascent indicates a yearning to reach a
higher plane of consciousness, while descent may point
to a quest for the unconscious. The regular motion of
climbing stairs or ascending and descending in an
elevator can stand for the sexual act.

Travel and transport

Dreams of undertaking a
long journey by land, sea or
air are often said to represent
a review of the dreamer's life
and goals. The hazards or crises
we encounter on the way through
life can appear as collisions,
breakdowns or barriers, while
dream destinations may
symbolize our aims
and achievements.

Road travel
Roads, with their twists, turns, forks
and crossroads, commonly represent
the journey through life, while
a horse or motor vehicle can
symbolize our energy and
motivation. If we are a passenger,
we may harbour a deep-seated sense
of being propelled through life by forces
of which we are not fully in command.

Aircraft

Dreams of air travel suggest a desire for a direct, smooth journey through life or some current difficulty. If the dreamer is the pilot, he or she is probably determined to be at the controls of destiny. An air crash should be heeded as a warning against overambition.

Trains

The raw power of the locomotive symbolizes vitality, and the fixed track suggests the single-minded pursuit of ambition. Missing a train reflects a fear of missed opportunities or of failure, while an attempt to alight from a speeding train points to a desire to take the pace of life a little easier.

Ships

The ship represents not just the dreamer's earthly career but also the greater journey toward spiritual fulfilment. Jung believed that ships could be vessels bearing the dreamer over the depths of the unconscious.

Pursuit and capture

Dreams of flight and entrapment can tell us much about the most pressing concerns of our psychic lives, as in the case of the man who could not shake off his mother's influence and dreamed that he was a swimmer being pursued by a great sailing ship. The message of such dreams is that there is one thing we can never escape from: ourselves.

Hunter and hunted

Being pursued by some creature suggests a preoccupation that refuses to go away – perhaps because we do not really want it to. If the dreamer is being followed but feels no threat, this could indicate a deep-seated desire to attract more attention or affection.

Spider's web

A cobweb is both the spider's home and a deadly trap: hence, the dreamer may be feeling pushed into a domestic arrangement (perhaps marriage). A spider can also represent fate spinning the thread of destiny.

Maze

The maze can be a classic symbol of the Self. If we find ourselves inside one, we may need to consider which psychological direction we are taking. At the centre of the maze (the heart of the Self) lies either repose or – as in the Labyrinth of Greek myth, the lair of the monstrous Minotaur – dark, subversive forces.

Prison

A dream of being in custody may express a sense of sexual or emotional repression. It could also suggest that the dreamer has a guilty conscience – an interpretation accepted by both ancient and modern dream analysts.

No way out

A path leading to a cul-de-sac or blind alley may be a recognition that some current concern is leading nowhere: we should pursue a more viable course. If we are being chased and find ourselves with no escape route, it could be time to terminate an obsession before it overpowers us.

The body

As the outer framework of the inner self, the human body yields a wealth of fundamental dream symbols. These may throw light on what Jung called "the inter-functioning of body and psyche", one of the keys to self-awareness.

Hair
Hair is associated with the head as a centre of spiritual power. It is also a symbol of sexual potency, so a man who dreams of going bald may fear loss of virility.

Eye
Believed in the ancient world to be the window of the soul, the eye symbolizes the mind and the light of understanding. Something stuck in the eye may represent sexual intercourse.

Skeleton
The skeleton is a traditional symbol of mortality but it can also denote spiritual liberation and renewal – the death of a barren phase of life.

Hand

Hands may denote creativity, though the left hand could refer to the dreamer's Shadow, or sinister, destructive urges. Dirty hands suggest feelings of guilt.

Teeth

In dreams, becoming toothless can reflect worries about the next phase of our lives and our strength to cope with its challenges and responsibilities. A man who loses his teeth may also fear castration, while a woman who swallows hers may be contemplating motherhood.

Clothing

In dreams, clothes reveal how
we truly see ourselves or our role
in life: someone who dreams of
wearing an elaborate headdress
may have a secret lust for power.
Stripped of our clothes, all our
vulnerability comes to the surface
– as anyone knows who has had
the common dream of being
naked in public.

Hats
Freud and others perceived the hat as a
classic symbol of the genitals. Whether the
male or female parts are meant depends on
whether the outside or the inside of the hat
is more prominent in the dream.

Uniforms
Being uniformed in a dream may reveal a tendency to be influenced too much by
the views of others, at the expense of one's own personality.

Shoes
The dreamer could be contemplating the next step in life. Shoes could also be a hint
about being realistic in one's goals – keep both feet on the ground.

Glasses

Glasses express a desire to see things clearly. If one of the lenses is broken, the dreamer is said to be undergoing some inner conflict.

Veil

A veil implies that some aspect of the person is not being fully revealed, either to the dreamer or to the outside world.

Coat or cloak

An overcoat or cloak suggests a need for warmth, security and protection, either from a loved one or from God. Analyzing one of his patients, Freud saw a coat as a symbol of protected intercourse and, indirectly, worries about pregnancy.

Clothes too short

This suggests a yearning for the innocence of childhood or for old pleasures now curtailed.

Commissioned artwork and photography